For the Early Birds' Garden Club—
every time we meet, you make life feel new.
—KP

RISE x Penguin Workshop

An imprint of Penguin Random House LLC, New York

First published in the United States of America by Rise x Penguin Workshop,
an imprint of Penguin Random House LLC, New York, 2022

Copyright © 2022 by Kari Percival

PENGUIN is a registered trademark and PENGUIN WORKSHOP is a trademark of
Penguin Books Ltd. The W colophon is a registered trademark and the RISE colophon
is a trademark of Penguin Random House LLC.

Visit us online at penguinrandomhouse.com.

Library of Congress Control Number: 2021014758

Manufactured in China

ISBN 9780593226797   10 9 8 7 6 5 HH

The text is set in BeoSans OT.
The art was created with silkscreens and collaged in Photoshop.

Edited by Gabriella DeGennaro
Designed by Maria Elias

HOW TO SAY HELLO TO A WORM

A FIRST GUIDE TO OUTSIDE

KARI PERCIVAL

RISE

NEW YORK

How do you plant lettuce seeds?

Sprinkle,
sprinkle,
sprinkle.

Pat, pat, pat.

Now make
some rain!

How do you say hello to a worm?

Gently, very gently.

Hello, Worm!

STRAWBERRIES

How do you plant peas?

Stick your finger in the dirt.
A hole!

Drop one pea in.

Give it a drink!

**Tuck all the peas
under the covers.**
Sweet dreams, Peas!

How do you say hello to a ladybug?

Let her crawl onto your finger.

Count her spots.

Say, *Hello, Ladybug!* before she flies away.

Have you ever seen so much green?

LETTUCE
FROST HARDY MIX

UTOPIAN VISION
SEED CO.

When will the peas sprout?

Shhh!
They are
still sleeping.

Good morning, Pea Sprouts!

How do you make mud?

Dig a path
for the water to go.

Make a river.
Flood it!
Mix, mix, mix.

Mmmmm! Mud!

Look! Pea plants!
See how they curl around your finger?
They want to climb!

Let's build a place for them
to keep growing.

Find some tall sticks.
Poke them into the ground.
Tie the top with string.
Ta-da! A play hut.
Now you can watch the vines
climb up, up, up!

How do you say hello to a bee?
Look but don't poke. See the pollen on her feet?
Listen but don't grab. Hear her wings buzzing?
If a bee mistakes you for a flower, hold very,
very still, and whisper, *Hello, Bee.*

But when will there be peas?

See how the play hut is shady?

See the flowers?

See the bees?

You'll see pea pods next.

How do you pick
a strawberry?

This one?
Not yet.
Too green.

This one?
Not yet.
Too white.

This one?
Not yet.
Too pink.

This one?
Not yet.
Too spotted.

This one?
Yes! Now!
That one!

Yum!

How do you pull a carrot?

A carrot? Where?

I don't see any carrots!

This carrot!

How do you pick peas?

Peas?
Yes!
Finally! Peas!

Find a pod.
Pop it open.
Look inside: peas in a row!
Dig one out with your finger.
Pop it in your mouth!
Yum!

Wow!
Look at all we've grown!
Has anything ever
tasted so sweet?

For Kids

Do you want to grow your own fruits and vegetables?

Here's what you'll need to grow a garden:

- seeds
- a sunny spot
- soil in a pot or garden plot
- water
- a grown-up to help

What should you grow?

Try growing some of your family's favorite fruits and vegetables, or the ones in this book, or even experiment with something you've never tasted before!

What's easy to grow and when will it grow best?

- **In cool, sweater-and-raincoat weather (55°F +) try strawberries, peas, lettuce, spinach, potatoes, kale, and radishes.**
- **In warm, T-shirt weather (70°F +) try carrots, beans, corn, squash, pumpkins, tomatoes, basil, and callaloo.**

For Grown-Ups

Why garden with toddlers?

Growing food empowers the very young. Gardening teaches about our connections with all the elements: the sun, the rain, our food, our bodies, the seasons, and the community of living things we belong to. It teaches patience and gratitude, and early memories of digging in the dirt help sprout a lifelong love of learning outdoors.

Is it worth the mess?

Get ahead of the mess by keeping things easy: wear shoes you don't mind getting wet, prepare a bucket of soap and water for a simple handwashing station, and have a towel and a change of dry clothes handy. This will help to keep things clean so you can focus on enjoying the simple pleasures of life together, stress free. So, yes—totally worth it.

What if kids want to dig and play in the plantings?

It's fun to keep a designated "dig zone" in the garden where kids can play freely in soil without disturbing seeds or young plants. Play is an important part of gardening! To separate the "dig zone" from the seedlings, create a noticeable border with plants like onions or pansies.

Is my child big enough to garden? How little is too little?

If your child is big enough to pull themselves up to stand using the edge of the garden bed, looks at the dirt with interest, and is curious enough to put their hand into the soil, then they are the right age to garden. Worried that curiosity will extend to your child wanting to taste test the soil? Have no fear! Follow the garden safety tips below to create a safe environment for your toddler to explore.

Garden safety!

Keep your garden safe for curious little ones by taking measures to reduce any health risks associated with ingesting soil:

- test your soil for lead ahead of planting
- protect your garden from pet and animal waste
- check for and remove any broken glass / harmful debris

And always have an adult present to encourage and help.